Helping Your Child Get Top Grades

Alan M. Solomon, Ph.D.,
and Penelope B. Grenoble, Ph.D.

CONTEMPORARY
BOOKS
CHICAGO · NEW YORK

ACKNOWLEDGMENT

Special thanks to Charlene Solomon, who worked on the original research for this book.

—PBG

Gratitude to Janet Suritzer, Ph.D., who has been a special mentor, supervisor, and colleague.

—AMS

CONTENTS

An Introduction to *ParentBooks That Work*

I t has been said that twenty-five-dollar words can
be used to cover up twenty-five-cent ideas. In our
increasingly technological society, jargon and complex language often confuse the meaning of information. This is particularly the case in the social and
psychological sciences.

The "hard sciences" such as physics, chemistry,
and biology have an advantage: there is little chance,
for example, that a photon or a quark will be con-
fused with something else.

In the human sciences, however, we have at least
two problems with language. One is that the popular
definition of a word such as *sex* or *intelligence* can
differ considerably from the way a professional in
the field might use it. Although we parents share a
common pool of language with social scientists and
teachers and therapists, words like *input* and
reinforcement, *expectations* and *assessment*, mean

one thing to parents and another to social science experts. Thus the danger that we will not understand each other is very real.

The human sciences' other language problem is jargon. A particular group of human scientists may develop obscure or seemingly incomprehensible language as a shortcut to communication among its members. Thus, jargon can be a roadblock when the experts try to talk to people outside their field.

The books in this series are the result of skillful collaboration between trained psychologists experienced in family and child development and a seasoned writer. The authors have strived to take twenty-five-dollar ideas and deliver them in language that is clear, concise, and most useful to you. In these six books, the emphasis is on presenting intelligent and practical ideas that you can use to help solve the age-old problems of child rearing.

This brings us to the very reason for these books. It might have occurred to you to ask, "Why should I rely on so-called experts when I can fall back on tradition and conventional wisdom? After all, the human race has survived well on what parents have taught children through the ages." Think about that for a moment. In the long history of human life on this planet, most of our energy has been spent in survival against the elements. It's only in most recent history that we've enjoyed the luxury to live, rather than simply survive. The fact is that the help and advice children need most nowadays has to do with a different level of survival in a world we've created ourselves, a complex world of rapid change.

Even though at moments nature can remind us of her often terrible wrath and power, most of our problems are still manmade. What we—parents and children both—have to learn is to deal with a reality that we have created ourselves.

In the bewildering array of cultures, creeds, and cross-purposes that are modern life, we need a special set of skills to live and be productive. Competition is an essential fact of life. Your child faces stress and pressure from society's expectations from the day he or she is born. To get through, your child needs the best help you can give.

The position of the professional expert is new and revered in our society. The expert is one of our cleverest inventions. Involved in the intense study of one problem or subject, the expert comes to know it better than anyone else. We trust the expert because we know that we don't have the time or ability to sort out everything ourselves. And, if the expert follows the best instincts of his profession, his high level of professional competence will serve you. By using the specialized knowledge of the expert, parents can face the difficult but practical problems of building a family and preparing their children to meet the demands of early childhood and elementary school.

Enlightened by this advice, we can give our children a healthy attitude and a better chance.

These concise and practical books deal with some of the most important issues in young children's lives today. They will help you to help your child and to feel good about your role as a parent. With this in mind, we dedicate this series to you.

Richard H. Thiel, Ph.D.
California State University

INTRODUCTION

One of the common misconceptions parents have about education today is that young children sent to school, who follow instructions closely and apply themselves diligently, will do well. Part of this is the belief that if children also receive the interest and support of their parents, they will be able to achieve the academic goals laid out for them. Even when their children are not doing well, parents generally tend to accept the wisdom and authority of the school system; they are often uncomfortable with probing deeper—first, because they trust our society's educational goals and the school system's ability to meet them. Second, they often may feel unprepared for challenging either.

A number of changes in our society, however, have caused many parents to lose sight of what *they* can do to help their children do well in school. The increase in two-career families, the high divorce rate, and increased career mobility can make a child's environment unstable, even chaotic. Overloaded by their own pressures, parents often shuffle children off to school, believing that there they will receive the necessary instruction and encouragement— sometimes ignorant of the problems children may have in adjusting to school or in learning a subject.

Many children experience some difficulty at various points in their school careers, due to a new curriculum, adapting to a new teacher or school, social pressures and family problems, or relatively weak academic abilities. It is the rare child who sails through school without some difficulty, at least on a short-term basis.

Unfortunately, you may have found to your dismay that the wisdom and enlightenment you counted on from your child's school may not be available. The problem is made worse by children's reluctance to talk about their school-related problems with their parents. Children may be embarrassed by feelings of failure, or they may sense that their parents are already burdened with other concerns. This is unfortunate, because many children really want to be able to talk with their teachers *and* their parents concerning school, and both parents and teachers want children to do well. The fact is that although a child's academic problem may not lie solely in the home, it is often in the home that solutions must be initiated.

An excerpt from *Educational Research Report,*

published by the *Congressional Quarterly*, sheds some light on the problems of our school systems.

> *We are all too aware of the statistics and reports emanating from a variety of official studies that America's classrooms are in crisis. Ever since April 1983, when a federal commission warned the nation of a "rising tide of mediocrity" in its schools, educators, legislators and the public in general have debated how to improve the quality of education in America. . . . The educational foundations of our society are presently being eroded by a rising tide of mediocrity that threatens our very future as a nation and a people.*

Strong words—ones to consider carefully because your child's future is at stake. Melodramatic? Not when you consider that high school graduates who can't read or make change are increasingly common and the college entrance exam scores of high school seniors have steadily declined.

More and more, parents are realizing that the "front line" for academic potential may not be in the classroom, but in the home. That is the premise of this book. You should seriously consider the possibility that if your child is not doing well in school, the problem—and the solution—may reside in your home.

We do not offer any simple or guaranteed methods to ensure that your child will be an *A* student or will excel in extracurricular activities. What we do offer are thought-provoking methods of considering his problems and talents and some practical solutions. It's a sure bet that in these pages you'll recognize some of the difficulties you might have experienced or are experiencing with your child. Remember, however, you are not alone; your child is not the only one who may be suffering difficulties . . . and from that knowledge take heart.

This book is divided into three parts. The first part presents an overview of the problem and a description of the factors related to your child's success in school. In the second part, systems for evaluating your child and his academic potential are suggested. Finally, Part Three presents recommendations for solving common academic problems. We are not concerned here with children who are undergoing severe academic difficulties, but with the average child who may be having some predictable problems navigating the shoals of education, especially in the primary grades. Although our concern is primarily with children between the ages of five and twelve, the logic of our recommendations can be applied to children entering adolescence and beyond.

As you read, you will find that this book goes beyond the issue of academic potential. When you consider it carefully, you'll notice that the material presented here also includes perspectives on family life and social situations, both of which are closely related to success in school.

We hope that this book will provide you with the opportunity to better understand your child's academic progress and help him enjoy a positive academic career. This is part of the happiness in life that comes with the realization that he has achieved his best.

While in this book we typically refer to a child using male pronouns such as he or his, please realize we are thinking of your daughter also. In contemporary society, academic achievement is as important to her as it is to her brother.

Part I
The Importance of Academic Skills and How They Develop

As we approach the end of the twentieth century, we are facing a society that has become increasingly competitive, with greater and greater rewards possible for those who strive for and achieve success. The stakes continue to increase, and very often the end is seen as justification for the means. Material rewards, particularly, are widespread in our predominantly middle-class society and are generally viewed as available to those of us whose aspirations are high and who are committed to our goals. Our society has evolved to the point where success is very highly valued and applauded. High levels of academic achievement and educational accomplishment are seen as essential to a successful life.

The quest for academic excellence begins in elementary school and continues through high school. College education is often considered mandatory and must be topped with a graduate school degree, often in a professional course of study such as medicine, law, business, or engineering. Although the goals of academic education were once less focused, and a college or graduate education was thought of more as finishing or rounding out the individual before he entered the world, today children—and their parents—tend to choose advanced courses of study that will be practical and enhance the child's future income.

OUR HIGHER EXPECTATIONS OF OUR CHILDREN

Because of higher demands of today's society, the focus on children's learning has increased in recent years. Responding to social pressure, parents tend to have higher aspirations and expectations for their children, and children themselves realize that there is more information to learn and more skills to master. Many parents expect more and more from their children at a much earlier age, and their children strive to respond.

A generation ago, for example, it was considered typical for children to begin reading in first grade. Kindergarten was a time for playing, for developing sensory motor skills, for doing arts and crafts, and for developing friendships. It provided children with a year of socialization before entering the more competitive world of structured learning. This scenario has changed, however. Now youngsters in kindergarten and even preschool are expected to learn their letters and numbers and to begin learning basic math skills . . . even to begin reading. Because parents' and teachers' expectations are much higher, the pressure on children, however subtle, is much greater. What we sometimes fail to realize is that while some children are ready to perform at these high levels, others are not. They are simply not yet ready to learn at this faster pace. If a child is pushed to learn before he is ready, he may end up with gaps in skill development or have a weakness in some subject area. Being pushed before he is ready can be a source of pressure and frustration for a child. The classic example occurs when parents are disappointed in a child who brings home a smattering of *B*s among the *A*s on his report card.

Instead of being rewarded for his accomplishments, the child may feel chastised and cheated. The fact of the matter is that *someone must be average.* Review of the results of a recent Wechsler IQ test sample indicated that 82 percent of the children tested fell into the overall average range. Forty-nine percent of the testees were considered average, while 16 percent were characterized as "bright-average" and another 16 percent as "low-average." Obviously not all children are smart enough to get straight *A*s, to graduate at the head of the class, or even to understand new math without a hitch. Your child does, however, have his own unique set of capabilities that can be identified and maximized. We all have areas in which we excel and areas of average or below-average performance. As adults we know that about ourselves and accept it; sometimes social pressure and our own aspirations as parents induce us to forget about this in regard to our children.

Thus the message of this book, maximizing your child's academic potential, refers particularly to the need for you to help your child discover where his relative strengths and weaknesses lie and then to help him enhance his strengths and accept and compensate for any weaknesses. You can diagnose achievement potential in your child and take specific steps to help him enhance his academic progress with the least amount of stress and optimum amount of satisfaction at the same time that you prepare him to compete in our intensely goal-oriented and demanding society.

Your expectations of your child are crucial in this process. A child forms his image of himself—and much of his image of the world—based on what he learns from you. Children are very skillful at picking up what you expect from them, whether or not they agree with it. Parental expectations that are positive will certainly help a child learn to aspire and reach goals. However, unrealistic expectations, especially ones that are inappropriate to the child's age, development, and individual skills, can intensify feelings of frustration and failure. Your child necessarily desires approval from you, and if he is constantly unable to achieve your expectations of him, he may fall into what we call "the failure syndrome." A child pushed to extremes can suffer from a number of serious problems, ranging from loss of motivation to psychological difficulties that may require professional help.

You know that you can be frustrated by your own inability to comprehend a new technology, whether it be a computer at work or your new stereo equipment at home. Imagine the frustration of a child forced to confront challenges for which he is unprepared—knowing that he must master this skill or complete that project according to his parents' predetermined standards.

UNDERSTANDING STRENGTHS AND WEAKNESSES

It is crucial that you understand what your child's strengths and weaknesses are and that you then develop an accurate, realistic estimate of his capabilities. As we indicated, some parents expect too much of their children. To accurately assess a child's potential, parents and educators should have a basic understanding of normal childhood development, which includes the various physical, intellectual, social, and emotional skills and behavior a child should be capable of at any given age.

It is also important that parents and educators understand that strengths and weaknesses are relative. A strength is an area where your child performs better than other children his own age or better than his own overall level of performance. Compared to his peers, for example, a child may be strong in reading, math, science, and baseball and have good social skills. Alternatively, a child may be strong in some areas and not in others—his reading, for example, may be better than his math. Conversely, a weakness is an area of relatively poor performance as compared to peers or the child's general level of competence.

This is the first lesson for you as a parent interested in helping your child get top grades: Listen to your own intuition and consider your own experience with your child before you attempt to apply the standards of other parents, teachers, or experts.

An understanding and accurate perception of your child's capabilities and motivations are crucial. Remember, if you're not accurate or truthful about his abilities, this can be extremely difficult for your child. All parents have some intuitive, usually unexpressed assumptions about child development. Asked casually about his child's behavior, for example, a parent will frequently put forth the explanation that this is a "stage" the child is going through. Intuitive understanding of the elements of child development is inadvertently expressed in this statement. The problem is that while many parents are actually aware of some significant stages of childhood growth and development, they frequently don't use this information correctly.

For example, most seven-year-olds are just beginning to develop conceptual skills. Parental efforts at an abstract discussion of a problem with a child of that age are probably inappropriate and may cause unwarranted anxiety in the child about his failure to understand what his parent is talking about.

Physical activity is another area that is often the focus of inappropriate expectations of children. The classic example is the Little League scenario, where parents expect an unrealistic level of physical coordination and strength from a child. There may be some children whose coordination is quite advanced and who are capable of strategizing in sports, but this is the exception more often than the rule. To judge your child's performance against that of the exception is to do him a gross disservice by pressuring what should be a normal developmental process.

Another problem that can often surface in our goal-oriented society is the parent who unknowingly attempts to experience success through his or her child. Perhaps the parent was slow in developing and did not experience the success he or she desired at an early age and thus wants the youngster to compensate for the parent's hurt or loss. Conversely, the parent may have been extremely successful as a youngster in some area and expects his child to emulate that success.

FACTORS INFLUENCING CHILD DEVELOPMENT AND LEARNING CAPABILITIES

Most parents realize that a child's ability to learn is not totally the result of his innate ability or talent. We live in an extremely complex society, and our children's ability to excel, combined with the interests they may choose to develop for themselves, are influenced by various and often complicated factors. Once you are able to isolate and understand some of these influences as they apply to your child, you will have taken an initial step in helping him maximize his learning potential. Following are several of those factors that influence the learning process.

1. The Impact of Television

Most of the recent research on television concerns the effects of violence. Unfortunately, there has been little, if any, research about the impact of TV on children's ability to focus on a task. Nonetheless, many teachers and therapists are very concerned that television—with its fast pace and visual stimulation—can condition children to expect the same rapid pace of stimulation in the structured learning situation of a classroom. TV can also condition children to passive learning, which leads them to experience difficulty in actively exerting themselves in a classroom and in interacting with their teachers and other children. Additionally, as TV-reared children grow older, they may have difficulty with independent learning situations where less entertainment is offered and more in-depth investigation is required. Working on book reports or other projects of some depth may be overwhelming. TV-conditioned children may experience difficulty developing such active learning techniques as thinking about and applying material they read or are otherwise exposed to. Applying a learned concept to a new situation can be difficult for such children; for example, word problems or math can be insurmountable.

You can help offset the TV syndrome by providing other avenues for learning and entertainment in your home—books, for example, for your child to investigate by himself or for the family to share together. Reading to children, even well into elementary school, can be an important first step in interesting them in independent investigation.

The effects of television aren't all negative, of course. Children today have access to a vast amount of information, especially with cable television and prerecorded videocassettes. An additional advantage is that this information is available to them on demand. This provides the opportunity for a child to review material on videocassette that he may not have fully comprehended when the subject was presented in the classroom. There are also more news and educational programs available on specialized cable TV channels; your family can take advantage of these as a unit, with you quizzing the children on what they see.

You are advised to steer your children to TV programming that is intellectually stimulating and demands interaction as opposed to programs that are strictly entertaining. Always remember, however, that you must weigh the benefits of television with the tremendous potential for difficulties that passive, visual learning may have for your children in later years. Limit their viewing. Watch with them at least sometimes so you can discuss programs with them. Actively monitor this source of influence.

2. Self-Esteem and Academic Achievement

Academic achievement is an enormous source of self-esteem, or feeling of well-being, for children. Adults tend to forget that children spend a good six hours of their day at school. This is a significant percentage of a child's productive time. Success or failure and how children see themselves in relation to their school activities—academically and socially— are very important factors in developing self-esteem. Adequate self-esteem is essential for academic achievement. Thus the two not only go hand in hand, but they are related as cause and effect. A child who

is not doing well in school, for whatever reason—
difficulty with a certain subject, inadequate communication with the teacher, inability to react to the
teaching methods used in a particular classroom—
will suffer a decrease in self-esteem, a frequent
symptom of which is depression. This discourage-
ment and loss of self-esteem will often lead to lowered motivation, less effort, and expectations of
failure.

A child who is repeatedly depressed, especially on
school days, may be trying to tell you something.
Even though he may protest that everything is fine at
school, and even though his marks may be acceptable, he may be suffering the cost of considerable
psychological and emotional effort. *Pay attention to
a child who appears to be "down" a good deal of the
time; attempt to ascertain the cause of his lack of
interest in things and, if need be, consider seeking
professional help.* For aid in drawing out a depressed
or withdrawn child, it may be useful to consult the
section on active listening in a companion book in
this series, *Creating Good Self-Image in Your Child.*

3. Motivation

One of the mistaken ideas about learning that has
become fundamental in our society—indeed to the
American way of life—is that sufficient effort will
produce success. The truth is that while motivation
is essential to achievement in any area, including
learning, it's not a guarantee. Likewise, lack of effort
isn't the only reason for failure.

In reality, your child's ability to meet learning

challenges may have nothing to do with his level of motivation. He may already be trying very hard but lacks skill in a certain area. As adults, for example, we can all recall difficulties with one subject or another—spelling or math, art or physical education—even though generally we might have been able to display a considerable amount of competency in our studies. Some of us may have excelled at spelling and composition while others struggled to make nouns possessive and verbs plural. Still others may have been math whizzes but couldn't draw a tree to save their soul.

Consider Elizabeth, a healthy twelve-year-old. She did very well in a rigorous, demanding private school, achieving all *A*s and *B*s. But by sixth grade her marks began to deteriorate; when she reached seventh grade her parents sought professional help because her grades fell to *C*s and *D*s. She even failed a science class. This happened despite her working very hard in school and devoting extensive time to her studies—spending as much as two to three hours an evening on homework. It seemed obvious that her academic problems were not a lack of motivation or effort. Elizabeth was a pleasant, well-behaved child, was attentive in class, and tried very hard.

After an evaluation by a professional, it became clear that there were glaring differences in Elizabeth's abilities: her memory skills were very strong, and her visual problem-solving skills were fairly strong—a little better than average for her age. But she had definite weaknesses in two areas, the first being the ability to express herself verbally. Elizabeth was quiet and rather shy. She could readily provide yes or no answers in a question-answer format, but she didn't do well when more open-ended discussion and elaboration were required. Additionally, Elizabeth had difficulties in comprehension and reasoning skills. If she had a task that involved memorizing, she could do quite well. She could easily memorize and recite poems; she learned all her early reading, spelling, and math skills easily. But she had difficulty drawing conclusions from the material she memorized.

But as each grade level required more understanding and reasoning, Elizabeth experienced increased difficulty. As a seventh-grader her reading comprehension skills were at a fifth-grade level. Despite being able to read and sound out seventh-grade words, she did not actually understand much of what she was reading. Her situation was complicated by the very academically oriented school she was attending, where most of the seventh-graders were actually comprehending at eighth- and ninth-grade levels.

Also, being rather shy, Elizabeth had more and more difficulty in the classroom because the increased number of lecture/discussion presentations by the teacher required more interaction from the students. There was less memory work and fewer work sheet assignments and more work that required the independent, conceptual learning skills Elizabeth lacked—taking notes in class, for example. She had trouble grasping the material, particularly in content areas such as science. Elizabeth could do well when the subject matter involved recalling facts, such as dates in history, but when it required reasoning, applying concepts, and inference, she performed poorly. She became discouraged about school and as a result was even more withdrawn and shy.

Elizabeth's therapist and her parents worked with the school staff and devised a plan where her teachers gave her somewhat easier materials with which to work. She was regrouped with children who were working at levels closer to her own. Her parents were encouraged to spend more time discussing school with her. Since her parents also tended to be rather quiet (which is how Elizabeth learned her behavior), they were encouraged to help her develop her discussion skills. They were asked, for example, to sit down with Elizabeth whenever she had a book report or had just finished reading a book and ask her to tell them about the story and its basic theme. They were asked to do more reading themselves and share with their daughter some of the basic themes in her books, not just the facts or chronology of events. They were also encouraged to watch specific television shows and use them as the basis for discussion, to examine what motivated the characters, to speculate on why they did certain things and what were they likely to do next, or to talk about other turns the plot might have taken.

And most important, Elizabeth's parents were advised to lower their expectations. While Elizabeth had been used to getting *A*s and *B*s earlier in school, her parents were encouraged to come to terms with the fact that in this school setting Elizabeth was likely to continue getting *C*s, with some *B*s. Although they had the option of changing schools, the family felt continuity was important and Elizabeth should remain at the same school. To combat the growing problem with her self-esteem, her parents made more effort to involve her with friends and steered her into joining a church youth group.

It is possible that Elizabeth may not be able to overcome some of her learning liabilities. As quiet as she is, however, she may be intimidated by the other, more verbal children in her highly competitive environment. If she fails to catch up and develop the skills she's lacking, her parents may be wise to revise their long-term expectations. When she is older they might encourage her to enter a junior college or an occupational program. If she succeeds on that level, she might gain enough confidence and skills to complete a four-year program of study.

If your child is experiencing difficulty in one subject, it should not cause despair and negativity about his overall abilities. *It's vital, however, that you understand where your child's relative weakness lies.* Difficulty in one subject should not lead you to believe that your child is academically weak overall. He will mostly likely be able to develop his own strengths as he grows, but he may need help compensating for his weaknesses. No amount of cheerleading to try to motivate a child to do better in an area where he is weak will be productive. It will only make your child more anxious about his failure. Apply your own enthusiasm to subjects in which the child shows proficiency and a desire to excel.

4. Innate Strengths and Weaknesses

The most important factor in helping your child

achieve maximum academic potential is to adopt a balanced approach toward your child's strengths and weaknesses. Many parents focus on their child's weaknesses. That's human nature, especially if your child has asked you to help him out, thus identifying for himself his own weak areas. If you have unrealistic expectations of your child, however, and he demonstrates a weakness in some area, you might become overzealous about fixing it, even though there may be little you can do except cause more anxiety in the child.

Let's take eight-year-old Joseph, for example. Joseph has a muscular problem that causes his eyes to cross. Eventually the condition will be corrected by several surgeries, but in the meantime Joseph has had to cope with a history of trouble in social relationships. He has developed few friends up to this point and has become overly sensitive about being teased. Typically, he reacts inappropriately by screaming and throwing a tantrum—which further isolates him from other students.

Joseph's parents are very concerned about this situation, as well they should be. Unfortunately, they are so involved with Joseph's problems that they have tended to overlook, or even downgrade, his considerable potential. This is extremely sad because Joseph is a very bright child. He reads well and is an able problem-solver. Although his usual behavior would belie it, Joseph actually has a sense of humor and, when he's relaxed, is quite adept at telling jokes.

Fortunately, Joseph's parents were so disturbed that they sought professional help. After he spoke with the child's parents, who described their son's problems in detail, the psychologist assessed Joseph's talents. It took a number of sessions, but the therapist was able to help Joseph's parents see—and become proud of—Joseph's abilities. Instead of constantly worrying about his difficulties with social skills—and making an issue of the occasions on which Joseph displayed inappropriate behavior—they began to spend time helping him further develop the things that he was good at, which in turn enhanced the child's rather lowered sense of self-esteem. Aiding Joseph to develop his positive talents will not only help him compensate for his physical disability; it will also help prepare him for more positive social interaction once his surgery is completed.

The lesson to be learned here is to take an inventory of your child's strengths and accentuate the positive; try to minimize the negative.

THE STAGES OF LEARNING

It is important for you to understand that children learn about the world in different ways, that not all children develop identical skills at the same ages, and that some children will develop some skills to a higher level than others.

Basically there are three ways by which we learn:

- through our senses;
- through perception, which involves recognizing objects and associations between them and expressing observations and conclusions; and
- through forming concepts.

Most children of the same age demonstrate different levels of development and ability as they mature. You will do well to observe your own talents, as well as those of other adults around you, as a constant reminder that each individual is unique and—if allowed and encouraged to do so—will develop a talent for learning that is uniquely his own. As we have pointed out previously, children differ in abilities; where one excels another may falter. Recognize and support the individual way your child learns about the world.

1. Learning Through Our Senses

An infant's first learning experiences are sensory, or what the experts call motor-kinesthetic. This simply means that infants move around and touch things. When you watch a small baby, you will notice that one of the first things he learns is how to grasp things with his hands. First he grasps, then he holds, then he lets go. Next he will use his hands to put things in his mouth. This series of events forms the primary source of learning in the first year or so of life. In this way a child learns what objects feel like, what their consistency is, how things change shape. Because the sucking reflex is the primary means of survival and satisfaction for an infant, it is natural that he subjects things to this "mouth test."

As the child begins to walk he begins touching and playing with objects. He will want to manipulate things. As most parents know so well, infants and toddlers often break anything that can be broken. The child is in the process of discovery and is developing his abilities and strengths.

A similar thing happens with emotions. Children at this age express their emotions behaviorally—frustration and anger may manifest themselves in tantrums, excitement and happiness as whoops or screams. An infant who cries seems to do so with his whole body.

As the child progresses to the next level of development, the sensory motor skills he has developed will remain with him. For example, when children learn to spell words, they often start by writing the words again and again. This is a motor means of learning. When preschool children are taught letters, teachers often show them large block letters made out of wood or plastic letters on magnetic boards. This helps the child manually manipulate the letters, but he also benefits visually learning about the shapes, making the process a multisensory learning experience. If children were only shown the letters, rather than having the opportunity to touch and move them, many would have difficulty, and some would be inhibited in their learning.

2. Learning Through Perception

The next stage of learning development involves seeing and learning, what the experts refer to as auditory and visual perception. It's important to note the distinction between sensing and perceiving. Sensations are the raw information that we take in from our surroundings—what we see, hear, touch, smell, and taste using the five basic senses. This information is useful only if it is organized by the brain. The mental process involved is known as *perception*.

We have auditory perceptual skills (what we hear) and visual perceptual skills (what we see). Frequently in early childhood the problem is organizing all the sensory information in the brain so that the sensations are understandable and so that the child can use the information to learn to perform tasks.

Doing well in reading, spelling, social studies, class discussions, and book reports usually means that your child is strong in seeing and hearing skills. These are tasks that involve listening and verbal expression skills. When you help such a child learn visual tasks—in subjects such as math, science, and geography—it's best to talk through the material. Your child will become more aware of the reasoning behind a math problem by talking his way through it. At an early level of development, you can also go back to sensory or motor skills. When your child is learning to do basic addition, subtraction, and even multiplication and fractions, for example, you might want to use concrete learning materials, such as counting sticks for addition and pies for fractions. It's unrealistic to go out and buy a pie every time you work with your child on fractions, but keep in mind that the next time you order a pizza or take home an apple pie from the store you can use it to reinforce what you are teaching the child. Visual cues may not be among your child's strengths, but if you have items for him to manipulate at the same time you're talking and reasoning with him, you're adding concrete motor reinforcement as well.

Very often children who have trouble with math do better when figures are translated into word problems. Reading a word problem requires the use of reading, comprehension, and auditory language skills. This is a more effective approach for the child than looking at figures in an equation, which uses very little of his natural verbal skills and may thus be frustrating to him.

Doing well in math or science, demonstrating a proficiency in drawing maps, understanding geography, developing and completing art projects, and solving puzzles and mazes typically means that your child is strong in visual, motor skills. He often has a good visual memory.

This type of child will likely do well in visual tasks. For example, when he begins learning to spell, such a child can visualize how the word looks when it's spelled correctly. He has an image of the word and knows when it looks right or looks wrong. Subsequently, when he writes the word or reads it on a page, he can check it against his visual memory.

As adults we all have our own little ways of remembering things. Each of us has his own methods when going into a grocery store to figure out what things cost. We develop these methods intuitively, without necessarily thinking about it or making a conscious choice. If you can help your child develop strategies in a more intentional way, he will learn to use his strengths when he gets into areas of difficulty. This is hard to do and often requires talking with a professional—the teacher—to come up with a solution. It also requires ingenuity and creativity. You are advised to spend time understanding the pattern your child uses in his attempts to remember and utilize information, For example, you might come to recognize that a strength of your child might be pretending or story-telling. Another child may have an avid interest in scientific areas such as the solar system or birds. If your child is a visual learner and doesn't like geography because it is taught to him solely by reading from a textbook and class discussions, you would do well to get him involved in maps and drawings of some of the material. He can make models, for example, of how different people around the world live. He can draw how these people dress or depict some of their customs. You can help your child master tasks by using creative techniques that apply his specific skills.

Although a child who is a strong visual learner is usually better in math, and one who is a strong auditory learner is probably better in reading and spelling, most subjects can be approached in a variety of ways that facilitate different learning styles. Science, for example, can be learned in a way that's more visual. Children can understand this subject by doing experiments, manipulating materials, and using charts and graphs—all of which are very visual. Or they can use a method that entails more reading, discussion, and verbalizing—all of which are auditory skills. Science for young children is usually a visual experience with lots of experiments and projects—things that can be done with the hands. Educators know that the best method for teaching younger children is to use a multisensory approach, which exposes children to kinesthetic, motor, visual, and auditory input. Combining different ways of learning provides the opportunity for children to utilize their individual skills.

Memory

Memory, like perception, is both auditory and visual. Children learn to remember what they hear and what they see. However, there are distinct differences among children in their memory skills. Some children remember very well whatever they hear. These children are generally good at listening to the teacher's verbal instructions and completing their work accordingly. Other children remember things when they see them. For example, math is largely a visual skill. A child who has good visual memory is likely to have good math skills. He's likely to learn arithmetical tables easily. It's as though there's an image in his mind that he can see.

Another child, who has good auditory memory, will memorize multiplication tables by repeating them to himself over and over again. An observer might even hear this child saying the tables softly to himself. The child hears the tables in his mind. He develops a rhythm and remembers whole tables that way. If you ask the child "How much is five times five?" he will start with five times one, five times two, and so forth. In this way he will have to run through the whole sequence. Though math is mostly a visual skill, the child with a strong auditory memory can adapt to the task.

Short-Term and Long-Term Memory. It's important to understand that there are two types of memory. Short-term memory is remembering something you've recently been exposed to. Long-term memory is remembering what you've been exposed to previously. Some children have excellent immediate recall. If you present information and teach them a basic math skill, they can remember it and do it well that day. Sometimes, though, by the next day they may not remember it because their long-term memory isn't as strong. Other children may have trouble with immediate memory but are able to recall the information or procedure long after it was presented to them. You should remember that children have different strengths and weaknesses in terms of short- and long-term memory; this is likely to be demonstrated in the progress your child makes in learning specific subjects. Also, memory is quite easily disrupted by anxiety or pressure. Thus stress can be quite detrimental to a child's memory skills.

3. Learning Through Concepts

Conceptual learning becomes very important as the child gets older and is certainly more essential later, in junior and senior high school. The more demanding many learning situations become, the more conceptual skills are likely to be required. You will want to be on the alert for a child who may do very well early in school, but has trouble later on because his conceptual skills may not develop very well.

Children with powerful conceptual skills can be very bright—geniuses even—but they might suffer from basic seeing and hearing problems. A child with such difficulties might do poorly in school with some of the basic tasks of reading and spelling, for example. This is often the case with a child who has what has been identified as a "learning disability." Your challenge with such a child is to prevent him from becoming so frustrated and consumed by failure that he gives up in school.

Conceptual skills involve two basic kinds of thinking. Reversible mental operations means that a child can think about something both "forward" and "backward." The second operation involves his ability to put things in categories.

The best example of a reversible mental operation is addition and subtraction. When your child can understand the relationship between addition and subtraction, he is thinking conceptually. Children can learn math in different ways, however. For most children, this reversible skill begins to develop at five and six, but it really becomes established at around seven. Learning can be either overt or covert. When a child stops having to count on his fingers, he has gone from overt to covert. He is able to *conceptualize* the relationship between the numbers without having to physically count out objects. This transition is also observable in the way children solve jigsaw puzzles. One child may employ a trial-and-error method, while another may scan the available pieces, study them, and then pick up the right one to put in the puzzle. The development of reversible mental skill varies tremendously among children. If a child isn't able to do some covert conceptualizing by ten or eleven, however, this is probably an indication of a potential lag in development. If a child at that age has to physically manipulate things and use an exhaustive trial-and-error approach when solving puzzles, this also may indicate a potential problem.

The ability to use categories is a more efficient

way of organizing or remembering material and a key to future learning. Most of us are bombarded with material constantly, and if we can't organize it into categories, it's hard to understand and make much use of the information. Without the ability to categorize, a child's efforts to remember things are impaired because he will jump from one subject to another without really understanding the information he's accumulated.

Using categories is really the result of developing rules. For example, children learn certain rules in multiplication tables. A child learns that to multiply by nine all he needs to do is add ten and take away one.

In this section we have provided an overview of the learning steps of childhood, as well as suggesting the importance of taking time to understand your child's learning progress and sharing in its development. We have also looked at some causes of learning problems. In the next section we offer some ways that you can help you child in his academic progress, regardless of the problems he may be facing.

Part II
Appraising Your Child's Learning Capabilities

There are several commonsense activities you can use to assess how your child is doing academically. Many parents overlook them and instead consider subjecting their children to unnecessary and troublesome tests and analysis. Spending time on the following activities is a fundamental first step for you to help your child maximize his academic potential.

1. OBSERVE YOUR CHILD'S INTERESTS

First and foremost, discover what your child naturally likes to do. Children tend to do things they enjoy and are good at. Aside from helping you determine your child's relative strengths and weaknesses, observing your child will help prepare you for the inevitable discussions about "what I want to be when I grow up."

When your child is six or seven, there's a variety of things he might enjoy. Favorite activities might be related to science or reading, or he might like someone to read to him. Some children focus on games involving numbers. Children of this age may like to play board games that involve play money or counting.

Equally important, observe what your child avoids. If he regularly avoids doing homework in a certain subject or has little to say about the subject when questioned about it, this might indicate that your child is experiencing some kind of frustration, fear, or weakness in that area.

Jacob, for example, was eager to do his book reports and raced through spelling practice. But he always left his math for last and complained that he was too tired to do it. Sometimes he avoided it completely. When he was forced to do math, his attention wandered, he asked for help, and he was easily frustrated. By observing their son carefully, Jacob's parents were able to determine that he was having some difficulty in math. If their observation had been spotty and superficial, they might have interpreted Jacob's enthusiasm for the subjects he likes as an indication that he enjoyed, and was doing well in, all of his subjects.

Although ideally you will be tuned in to your child from the time he is born, observation that is designed to assess his potential should take place over a substantial period of time, certainly longer than a single day or week. It may require several weeks to observe some pattern(s) in your child's activities or preferences.

If you find your child is not doing well in a specific area, do not become alarmed or cajole the youngster into performing until additional research is done. One of the primary places to secure help in this effort is the school and the child's teacher.

2. OBSERVE HOW YOUR CHILD LEARNS

Observing your child's preferences is more than a simple assessment of his likes and dislikes about subjects or activities. If you know something about *how* your child learns, you can better gauge his strengths and weaknesses and help institute a program to further develop strengths and compensate for weaknesses. For example, a second- or third-grader usually is developing reading skills. Determining your child's style of reading will help you understand his primary learning technique. You will then be able to determine whether the style of teaching used in your child's classroom is compatible with his skills. If there is a problem, you can take steps to compensate for what the child may be missing in school.

First, notice whether your child is able to sound out new words. Can he break down words into syllables? Can he figure out the sounds of the letters? Can he put those sounds together? If he uses these phonetic methods, he's working with hearing, or auditory, skills and is probably an auditory learner. Or it might be that he prefers to visually recognize the word as a whole. If he's working that way, he's using visual memory to learn words.

Generally, reading is an auditory skill. Once past early primary readers the words become longer, the sentences usually are more complicated, and the material is more complex. This is where the development of auditory skills is important. If your child is having trouble breaking down words into parts and figuring out the sounds, he might find it difficult to keep up with the class.

Your child's approach to spelling may be another indication of his learning skills. If he spells by sounding out or subvocalizing (saying the word to himself in syllables), he may be a strong auditory learner. On the other hand, he may close his eyes to try to visualize the word to see what it looks like and thus be using visual memory.

Some children try to use both methods. They sound out a word and then also look at it to see if it looks right. Some children will say, "That word doesn't look right to me." That child is using both visual and auditory memory skills. A child with good visual memory may learn spelling by writing the words. He's using both visual and motor skills. A child with good auditory memory will learn by sounding them out.

Having watched your child to see what his interests are and how he learns and remembers things, there are three follow-up activities that you should complete.

3. EVALUATE THE LEARNING TECHNIQUES IN YOUR CHILD'S CLASSROOM

It's very important to keep in touch with your child's primary teacher. At the beginning of the school year arrange for a conference and perhaps include your child for part of it. Explain any concerns you have and be sure to let the teacher know any observations you have made about your child and any changes you have seen in your child's preferences over the years. Also apprise the teacher of any problems your child may have that you have already noticed. After the teacher has gotten a chance to know your child—say, in about six weeks or so—it's a good idea to set up another meeting.

At this second meeting it is the teacher who should do most of the talking. Solicit his or her opinion on how your child is doing, in which areas he is successful and demonstrating skills and in which he is having problems.

Remember, you want to know about successes as well as failures. As always, bring to the teacher's attention what you observe about your child at home, such as unwillingness or inability to discuss school or do homework, and any new or unusual personality traits that seem to be developing.

Perhaps your child's teacher will be overly enthusiastic, praising your child and indicating general competence: "Jeremy is so good at everything! I wish all the children in my class were like yours." Enjoy the praise and success and then ask the teacher to be more specific about what your child does that is so delightful. Ask for examples. Solicit his or her opinion about what makes your child so successful. In other words, it is as important to know why your child is doing well as it is to know why he may be doing poorly. If the teacher can explain the reasons to you, he or she will be better able to take advantage of your child's positive traits and perhaps be less frustrated by his negative ones.

Ask to see samples of the work your child has done in the classroom. Compare progress with work that has been done in the past. Assess whether he really is progressing or is actually more at a standstill. Make sure not only that the teacher is accurate, relative to your observations, but that his or her expectations are realistic. The teacher might say that your child is absolutely wonderful, but you may observe that the work he is doing is at a level similar to that of the previous year. Maybe the teacher isn't expecting enough, or the general level of the class may be lower than your child is used to. Additional work or a regrouping with children from other classes who are more advanced than many of those in his classroom might be required.

The following is a sample conversation between informed, concerned parents and their child's teacher. We include it to give you some suggestion of how you might want to approach your own child's teacher and of what you might expect when you do.

Teacher: *Your child is a joy to have in our first-grade classroom, Mr. and Mrs. James. I wish every student were as pleasant as he is.*

Dad: *Thank you. We always love to hear that.*

Mom: *What makes him so pleasant in class?*

Teacher: *Well, he's kind to the other children, and he seems to be good at most everything.*

Dad: *That's wonderful. We value good social skills in our family. Can you tell me what he seems especially interested in?*

Teacher: *Let me see. He's really not a problem, so sometimes it's hard to tell. I have my hands full with kids who really need my attention.*

Mom: *Of course you do, but we'd like to know what you see as some of Andrew's special talents so we can encourage them at home.*

Dad: *We know that he loves to play card games.*

Teacher: *Yes. He's very good at math, and that shows up in playing cards. He's been trying to learn to play chess with one of the older kids who comes in to help in the classroom in the afternoon.*

Dad: *Is there anything you think we can do with him at home that would encourage him?*

Teacher: *I think you could get him some math games—but try to stay away from those pencil-and-paper workbooks. Children like Andrew often burn out on work sheets by the time they're in the fourth grade. They've had so many of them by that time.*

Mom: *Math games sound good. Do you have any specific ideas?*

Teacher: *Not especially, but anything that involves counting or grouping of numbers will be fun for him. The curriculum materials store in town has a good selection. And also, you can call the museum to see if they have any special classes that you think he'd like.*

Dad: *Thank you. That's an excellent idea.*

Teacher: *I think the most important thing with a child like Andrew is for you not to pressure him. Encourage him to have fun while he's learning. He'll certainly pick up whatever else he needs from school. But you don't want to make learning unpleasant by pushing him too hard.*

Mom: *Thank you for your suggestions. We'll give them a try.*

4. ASSESS YOUR CHILD IN RELATIONSHIP TO HIS PEERS

It's important to assess your child's strengths and weaknesses relative to other children, as well as to himself. If he has somewhat more limited abilities in some areas, then average performance in those areas is reasonable. Not every child will grow up to be a bank president, even though his parents might wish him to be.

Weakness can be seen in two ways: first, in relation to other children your child's age, determined through nationally based norms on IQ tests, for example; and second, in relation to his own personal strengths.

An easy way for you to undermine your child's confidence is to focus on his weak areas and neglect superior skills. Your child may not actually be weak in reading; he may be average. However, if he has above average skills in math, he may appear to be *relatively* weak in reading if he is only on an average level. You will do well to remember that the ability to work at grade level is an important accomplishment. Penmanship for boys is often rough because fine motor skills are less developed in boys compared to girls. Emphasis on neatness beyond a reasonable degree may be a source of feelings of failure for a boy.

5. BE ALERT TO SPECIAL TALENT THAT YOU MAY BE ABLE TO TAKE ADVANTAGE OF

Some children may be athletically gifted but not academically inclined. Usually these children will eagerly and strenuously pursue athletics and neglect their area of weakness—academics. Unfortunately, this kind of child may grow up to be a professional athlete but never really develop the intellectual skills necessary for a balanced life. Additionally, because only a very few athletically capable children will go on to become successful professional athletes, parents and teachers should be prepared to help them develop alternative means of supporting themselves as adults. This is more of a challenge than it may seem since many athletically inclined children really don't like academic tasks.

For example, Scott, a fifth-grader, is gifted at Little League baseball and soccer, but he is not doing well in his academic subjects. Scott's parents, aware of the problem, consulted with his teacher, who proved to be very helpful. She pointed out that because Scott is so athletic he is also very popular, especially with the boys in his class. She also noted that one subject that Scott was doing well in was art, and she suggested to his parents that he incorporate this skill in learning other subjects. Now when Scott has an assignment in social studies and reading, drawing is made a part of it. He was encouraged, for example, to include drawings in his reports. To make the academic work a little more interesting to him, his teacher also suggested that he read sports-related stories, choose spelling words associated with sports, and if he's required to do a book report, that the book be on athletics. It took a little time and some perseverance to implement this program, but it seems to have paid off. Even Scott's science projects are now taken from sports; he has done research and written papers, for example, on what makes a baseball curve and on what atmospheric conditions cause a baseball to travel longer versus shorter distances. This channeling of Scott's interest in athletics into academic areas related to sports might even suggest a career choice for Scott as he grows older.

Another example is Suzanne, who is in third grade and is very interested in art and drama but generally doesn't do well in other subjects. After her parents met with her teacher and consulted with her pediatrician to be sure that Suzanne wasn't suffering from a physiological ailment, they decided to become actively involved in using her strengths to help her compensate for her weaknesses. To strengthen her reading skills, they encouraged her to select plays to read. They read with her as a family, encouraging her to take one or more of the parts. After taking her to a number of art shows, they read biographies of some famous artists whose work they had seen. Suzanne slowly grew more attentive in school.

Once an accurate assessment of Scott's and Suzanne's problems had been made, their parents could see how to help their children. This is the case with most children. Occasionally there is another cause for failure to achieve academically that isn't easily seen and requires different, stronger action.

There are some children, for example, who have a short attention span that has developed into what we call *attention deficit disorder*. This is a condition that can be severe enough to cause learning problems. Such children find it difficult to sit and focus on a subject or problem. If you suspect your child is having a very difficult time paying attention in class or at home, you should seek professional help; the sooner the problem is noticed, the better. The condition usually becomes obvious in early elementary school. Such children are frequently quite bright, and if they get help early enough, they are often able to catch up.

Children who don't have as severe a problem can be helped by your providing increased structure in the home environment that makes it easy for the child to focus.

Jennifer, for example, is ten years old; she is a pleasant, likable child—cute and charming but a bit disoriented and at loose ends. Her teacher reported that she seemed to be "in outer space" when she was sitting in class. If she did eventually begin a project, she would soon drift off and accomplish very little. By the fifth grade Jennifer was barely keeping up. Although it appeared that she was of at least average intelligence, her work was classified as low-average. When she did become more actively involved in something, however, she was productive and could easily do fifth-grade work.

A parent-teacher consultation indicated a pattern that was evident at home and at school. As Jennifer moved through elementary school, she tended to do less well as the classroom situation became less structured and more independent work was expected of her. In the upper grades a classroom assignment might require ten to twenty minutes of independent work and involve little interaction with the teacher. Jennifer just couldn't work steadily for that length of time. She'd get five minutes into the assignment and drift off. Her parents found the same was true at home. Jennifer would sit down to do homework, and in a few minutes she'd be staring off into space or get up from her desk and move around the room.

Eventually Jennifer's parents and teacher set up a program of checking on her work at home and in school. This required checking her progress at approximately five-minute intervals, an attention span that seemed to apply to most of Jennifer's subjects, including spelling, arithmetic, and science (all except art, which was pure pleasure for her). Using this program, Jennifer's teacher and her parents would simply pat her on the back if she were able to concentrate for five minutes and urge her to continue. If her attention had wandered, they would redirect her back to the task and then check with her in another five minutes.

Gradually, the intervals were expanded to six minutes and then seven minutes. Over a few months Jennifer's attention span slowly began to increase. She was able to focus on her work for longer periods of time. Her parents also found that her attention varied tremendously depending on how well rested she was. So they made it a priority to insist that Jennifer go to bed at a reasonable hour and have a good night's sleep, even though Jennifer usually resisted their efforts. They also found that Jennifer's lack of ability to concentrate for longer periods of time coincided with the birth of a baby sister, which had made her parents less available to her. Jennifer and her parents discussed this element of the problem, and her parents assured Jennifer of their love for her and their commitment to her.

After you have identified some of the potential problems that might inhibit your child's ability to do well in school, the next step is to use the strategies suggested in the following chapter. Some of these suggestions may seem obvious to you, simply a matter of common sense. It's amazing, however, how many families neglect the obvious. We have tried to present as many practical alternatives as possible, solutions that have worked for other children and can work for yours.

Remember to take the time to observe your child's interests over a period of time and to understand how your child learns. Visit your child's school and evaluate the teacher's learning techniques. Be particularly careful to observe your child's relationships with his peers. (You might want to consult a companion book in this series, *When Your Child Grows Up Too Fast*, for a discussion of the importance of social skills in developing children.) And finally, always watch for any special talents your child might have so that you can help him take advantage of them.

Part III
Specific Strategies for Helping Your Child In School

In our complex world we are constantly bombarded by activities and challenges that require attention and action. Because most of us often feel we have more demands on our time than we can handle, we have been as specific as possible in this fourteen-point program for helping your child maximize his academic potential. Whenever possible we have provided sample dialogue for you to use with your child and/or included mini-case studies showing how other children and their families have faced similar challenges.

Listen to your own intuition about your child and consider your experience with him before you attempt to apply standards of other parents, teachers, and experts or achievements of other children. To do this you must first be involved with your child and be aware of your own anxieties about your child's abilities. You must eliminate stress and provide structure in family life and at school, if necessary. You must learn to help your child cope with mistakes. You must praise your child when he does well and think of special activities that help him do so. Finally, you must continuously work at enhancing his self-esteem. The time you spend with your child in these and other efforts will be rewarding for both of you and will give you the added satisfaction of providing your child with the best possible start in life.

Let's look specifically at what each of these recommendations is about.

HELPFUL HINT #1—BE INVOLVED

Your involvement in your child's learning process is perhaps the most essential element in the learning equation. When you are involved in your child's school activities, it gives him the message that you care. *This is the most important message you can convey.* Your lack of involvement says to your child, "I don't care how you're doing. I don't make time to meet with your teacher or monitor your activities because it just doesn't matter that much."

Sometimes parents find it difficult to be deeply involved with their children's school because of heavy time commitments of their own. This is often the case in single-parent families and in families where both parents work. However, some degree of involvement is basic to your child's success in school. There is just no way around it. A nanny or baby-sitter or other form of household help is not the same. Your child benefits by knowing that *you* care. Remember also, however, that you must beware of caring too much. An overly solicitous parent can create anxiety in a child. If you feel that this may be a problem in your family, you may want to consult the section on overindulged children in the companion volume *When Your Child Grows Up Too Fast.*

If you are involved, you're telling your child that you care, are concerned, and love him. This involvement can take place casually—in a dinner discussion, when you take a minute for a few questions at breakfast before the child leaves for school, or when he comes home and is winding down. It can take the form of questions or comments about a classroom project you know your child is working on. And it can be especially rewarding to the child if you take the time to actually look at some of the work he has done in class or routinely, but casually, review his homework. (When we say "casually," we are assuming that he has no *basic* difficulties with homework. We will discuss that problem in detail as we proceed.)

Recently a group of researchers investigating significant factors in academic success concluded that one of the most important ones common among children doing well in school was quality time spent together in the family unit—when parents and children take the time to talk to one another about the things that are going on in their lives. The study concluded that if the interaction is sufficiently relaxing, enriching, and stimulating, it encourages children to open up and talk about school. This also shows children that their parents are concerned and involved in their world . . . and are ready to offer help and guidance if needed.

As we suggested previously, this kind of interaction may take place over dinner (it's amazing how many families do not eat even one meal a day together) or at an extracurricular activity centered around the child: Little League, Scouts, etc. Or it may be part of family-oriented leisure-time activities: biking, sports, or something as simple as walking around the block together. Finally, it may be focused around a school-sponsored activity: a play, an athletic event, an open house, or a teacher-parent conference night.

HELPFUL HINT #2—KNOW YOUR CHILD'S TEACHER

Sometimes it's essential to be very specific with your child's teacher. Once you have met the teacher and told him or her of your interest in your child's well-being, you might ask about specific subjects. As we have already suggested, you might ask, "What subject is my child having difficulty with? What material is he working on?" You might request a sample of your child's classroom work. Above all, you should share your own observations with the teacher. If the teacher is reluctant to tell you about difficult behavior on the part of your child, but you show you're willing to be open, it will be much easier to talk. This way you can work together to find out what's causing your child's problems.

As the teacher makes observations of your child and tells you about them, you can combine them with your own sense of your child's weak and strong points and be in a much better position to help. Don't forget, however, that a teacher has an entire classroom of children to deal with, and it's a mistake to think that all of your child's difficulties can be solved solely in the classroom.

Let's take Justin, for example. He is a fourth-grader who is having trouble with arithmetic. He was able to do fairly well in the subject when it involved addition and subtraction, but he developed difficulty with multiplication tables. Justin's teacher pointed out to his parents that Justin couldn't seem to memorize the tables. Because Justin appears to have weak visual skills, working with paper, pencil, and flash cards was not the best way for him to master multiplication. Justin's parents and teacher discussed other alternatives until finally a solution was developed using Justin's stronger auditory skills. Justin was urged to memorize and recite the tables verbally; he learned the tables as a kind of song. Of course, there is some difficulty in this system in that when Justin needs to know what the answer to four times four is, he must run through the fours up to that point. It's a slow method, but it is a good way for a child such as Justin, with slowly developing memory skills, to keep up with other children his age. And eventually, after he practices a lot, Justin will be able to *visualize* four times four without running through the whole table. The process is slow and cumbersome, but it gives Justin a sense of accomplishment. This in turn enhances his sense of self-esteem. His feelings about himself might become negative if he fell behind the rest of the class.

You must of course realize that not all teachers can and want to work with students so intensely. Some are short on time. Some are comfortable teaching only according to a set method. Most often teachers have large classes, which makes it difficult for them to offer individual instruction. If this happens, there are other things you can do. You can:

● Ask other parents what has worked for their children with similar learning problems.

● Seek out a special curriculum store and talk with the staff. Knowing your problem, a staff member is likely to be able to suggest an alternative learning method—a game, for example, that you might not even be aware of.

● Investigate other in-school help. Talk with the principal to see if you can set up an appointment with a learning resource specialist if one is available.

● Check in your neighborhood for tutorial services. Tutors can be an excellent source of assistance. You might find a professional source or even a high school or college student who is willing and qualified to come to your house. For more information on what you can expect from professional help, as well as suggestions on how to choose the right person, you might again wish to consult the companion volume *When Your Child Grows Up Too Fast*.

HELPFUL HINT #3—BE AWARE OF YOUR OWN ANXIETIES

It is not unusual to see anxiety in parents when they talk about their children's capabilities with other parents. Sophie, for example, often compared her daughter, Megan, with the other children in Megan's second-grade class. Megan was bright, but she had some difficulty in spelling and reading. Whenever Sophie talked with the other parents about their children, she came away feeling increasingly anxious and worried about Megan's abilities. To calm herself, she would speak briefly with Megan's teacher, who took pains to reassure her that Megan was doing fine, although only a little slow in language arts.

Regardless of the teacher's reassurances, however, Sophie continued to worry that there was something wrong with Megan. Unfortunately, this was a case where a mother was actually hurting her child and herself. You should be extremely cautious in listening to another parent's view of a child's performance or capabilities—be it your child or his. Ask yourself, "Does this parent have reasonable expectations for his child? Is he a good source of information?" Don't just accept or reject what he or she says. Evaluate it in light of your own anxieties, which will affect the way you take the information. The old adage says the sins of the father are visited on the child, and likewise so may be his insecurities and anxieties.

In most cases, your own intuition and observation of your child's ability are more important than outsider's opinions. Obviously, if you are emotionally upset about your child's performance, then other, impartial views will be important to think about. And, in this case, the outside input should be that of an experienced professional.

HELPFUL HINT #4—THINK ABOUT YOUR EXPECTATIONS OF YOUR CHILD

If you feel the least bit unsure about the level at which your child should be performing at his age, ask his teacher. Ask the teacher to tell you how he or she thinks your child is doing compared to what he is *expected* to be doing at his age. At the same time, you might do some reading on child development to determine whether *you* might be expecting too much.

Remember, you must recognize and be sensitive to the areas of relative weakness and strength in your child. After all, you are not raising a robot. Not all children will do well in all areas. It's the rare child who can make outstanding accomplishments in all subjects. For some children a grade of *C* in a subject area may be a reasonable expectation. If young Justin, whom we spoke about earlier, can manage a *C* in math when it involves multiplication, his parents have learned not to be distressed. They understand that he's working to the best of *his* capabilities—and math is not his best subject. They also understand that to expect more and put pressure on Justin may create frustration and anxiety for the child—and for themselves. Even worse, Justin may end up doing poorly in all of his subjects. He may also face a larger problem—the feeling that he is a failure. In either case, the result will cause friction in the parent-child relationship.

You should not expect that because you excelled in reading or math your child will do the same. It's important to have realistic, objective expectations, considering your individual child's capabilities. Just because a mother is a professional concert pianist, for example, doesn't mean that her daughter is going to be skilled at the keyboard.

HELPFUL HINT #5—AVOID PRESSURING YOUR CHILD

If you know what your child's capabilities are and can accept them, you will be less likely to put unnecessary pressure on your child and yourself. A common situation in upper-middle-class and upwardly mobile families is the need to excel. A grade of *B* or *C* is often considered failure, even though it may mean the child is working at full or close-to-full potential.

How can you reach the point where you accept that your child is performing his best in any subject? After you've observed your child for a reasonable amount of time—several weeks or even months—

you will begin to see a pattern. You will begin to see that he is stronger in certain areas and weaker in others. *You should strive to take delight in those areas in which he excels, even though they might not reflect your particular skills or expectations.*

For example, one of the important skills children develop in first or second grade is penmanship, which requires fine motor skills and hand-eye coordination. There are, however, activities related to fine motor skills that you can observe even earlier: coloring, cutting, and pasting—the arts and crafts activities of many nursery schools and kindergartens. Some children don't have well-developed fine motor skills. They may have good *gross* motor skills—riding a bike, throwing, catching a ball, running, or skipping—but the fine motor skills are not well developed. If you have been observing your child carefully as we have advised you to, you will notice this slower development of fine motor coordination early on, and you will not be surprised when the child has difficulty with penmanship. It is when you don't pay sufficient attention to your child, that anxiety may develop when he unexpectedly can't complete a task or demonstrate a particular skill.

No matter how hard he tries, your kindergartner or first-grader may not produce neat work compared with other children his age. This is frequently a problem with boys. Girls often have better fine motor skills and are encouraged to have the patience and the passivity to practice this kind of task. Girls frequently develop earlier as well. By the end of kindergarten, if your child is able to produce passable writing, that may be sufficient.

Seven-year-old Danny, for example, isn't very good at drawing or writing. His father, Sam, on the other hand, is an architect who dreams that Danny will follow in his footsteps. The therapist who was working with Danny and his father on this problem suggested that Danny's father realize that his son may not have the abilities in this area that he wishes him to have. Although Danny's fine motor skills are poor, he is very good at reading and language arts and wants to participate in these activities. It is of course risky to predict that a child of seven will never develop the skills to become an architect. However, it's even riskier to say "I want my child to develop the skills that I have." This may cause intense conflict and frustration between the parent and child and within the child himself.

In such a case, you should establish reasonable expectations and relax some of the pressure. That doesn't mean that you should accept sloppy, terrible work, but you can develop reasonable goals for your child by talking with his teacher. These goals might be hierarchical, that is they will gradually implement an accelerated program of expectations. This process of gradual improvement can also help your child in other ways. For example, Danny's parents helped him learn to use a computer to do some of his written work. He did his spelling words, written book reports, and compositions on the computer to eliminate some of his penmanship problems and the anxiety they created.

Children often become more interested in working on book reports and other language arts activities when a typewriter is made available; handwriting the reports is no longer frustrating. In fact, the thrill of using a computer or typewriter helps to motivate a child to become interested in writing. It's also a great way to teach spelling because when a child works on the keyboard he has to spell out words more slowly, letter by letter.

When your child is working on a book report or other project, however, you should allow him to complete the report and provide help only when asked. Later, if your child suggests it, you can discuss corrections and editing with him. Again we are assuming there are no gross problems with either. This has to be done with care, however. Parents sometimes have a tendency to overcorrect or correct their child's work in a harsh way. Avoid sharp criticism and explain your corrections. Take time to do this. Limit the number of corrections you make.

Another option is allowing your child to dictate the book report, story, or science report. This lets him do some of the work but eliminates the handwriting problem. You can't neglect handwriting completely, however. You should decide with the teacher on a minimum level of skill that's acceptable for your child. The difficulty that parents have is understanding that a child can be very bright and talented but still have considerable difficulty in writing.

For some children of six or seven you can attempt to bypass some of the problems with printing by switching to a cursive program. You should, of course, consult your child's teacher about such a step. Children sometimes find that cursive writing goes more quickly, is more satisfying, and looks better and are therefore more motivated to do it.

For a child who has difficulty writing, initial work at spelling and writing may appear crude or messy and full of erasures. Spacing may be a problem. Be patient. Be understanding and learn to be satisfied with the best he can do. And most of all, don't keep him from his soccer practice to practice his penmanship. He already knows that he's having trouble in that area. *Give him the opportunity to do something that he can feel good about.*

Although lengthy, this discussion of penmanship problems conveys the importance of moderating pressures on children. The example of how to evaluate, accept, and solve penmanship problems should be applied to your child's own particular difficulties.

HELPFUL HINT #6—HELP YOUR CHILD LEARN TO COMPENSATE

Once you know your child's areas of relative strength and weakness—which requires continuing observation because it is an ever-changing process—you can help your child use his strengths to make up for his weaknesses. Adults do this all the time. For example, when someone plays tennis and has a stronger forehand than backhand, he usually will position himself on the tennis court to try to take advantage of the forehand.

Jeffrey is eleven. He doesn't have a particularly good auditory, or hearing, memory. His strength is in motor skills. He's athletic, good in sports, and likes to ride his bike. He also has fine motor skills and likes to do activities such as drawing and working puzzles. He's very good in handwriting, and he's good in math. But he's not strong in spelling and reading. When he's involved with discussion groups, which usually begin to occur more frequently when children reach the age of ten and eleven, or receives more complicated homework assignments, Jeffrey has trouble.

Since he has trouble with auditory memory skills, Jeffrey does better with written work than with discussions in class where he finds it difficult to express himself and understand what the teacher is saying. Eventually Jeffrey learned that to do his best he must take notes. During discussion sessions and when the teacher is explaining things, he writes down the key things the teacher says. Then he doesn't have to rely strictly on listening and trying to remember. Also, if he takes notes, Jeffrey is translating lessons that are auditory into ones that take advantage of his motor and visual skills. In effect, he's creating a stronger way of learning for himself. Teaching Jeffrey how to take notes was very important . . . and it was his parents who taught him how to do it.

Jeffrey's parents talked with him and helped him develop ideas about taking notes in class. They gave him a homework pad to keep assignments and write down specific directions about work to be done. They encouraged him to use his homework pad and praised his efforts when his work was done correctly.

Another example of a child who has learned to compensate is nine-year-old Tiffany, who unlike Jeffrey has strong auditory skills. She's very good in reading and spelling, and she's able to listen and follow directions. Tiffany easily participates in discussions in class and at home. She has good social skills. But she has trouble with math. To alleviate her problem she learned to recite the multiplication tables. She can do it to herself subvocally (in her mind), and when she's doing more complicated math problems where rules have to be followed she can verbalize the rules out loud.

For Tiffany, writing facts down might not help much, but writing them along with verbalizing, or talking them through, helps tremendously. After repeating instructions out loud, she then goes though them in her mind so shc can repeat to herself what she's learning as she works. Thus she says to herself for a multiplication problem, "I start at the right-hand side of the problem, and the number goes here. Then I move to the second column, and the number goes there."

When Tiffany's parents work with her on math, they help her to remember that this verbalizing is important. They show her exactly what needs to be done. When Tiffany started this kind of activity, her parents would sit with her and literally repeat the math problems with her over and over again. They supported and rewarded her and they continually praised her.

Billy, however, is a different type of child. He is six years old and in the first grade. Since preschool Billy has indicated an interest in learning numbers. Billy's grandfather taught him to play blackjack when he was three, and this became a basis for learning arithmetic skills such as counting and adding. Even in preschool Billy was doing simple addition, and he was learning something about subtraction by the time he started kindergarten.

The problem was that Billy's handwriting was not the greatest. It wasn't terrible, but it wasn't nearly as developed as some of his other skills. Billy loved it when people read to him and was able to recognize all the letters by the time he was in kindergarten. But he just didn't develop quickly in reading or spelling. Billy's recognizing sight words—the first small words that children pick up—was about average for kindergarten level. He didn't read as fast as some of the others in the class, even though his math continued to develop very strongly.

This situation was difficult for Billy's parents to accept because both highly valued reading. In fact, Billy's mother was a literature major in college, so it was even more important to her that Billy do better in reading. Both parents became increasingly anxious and uncomfortable with Billy's lack of skill in reading compared to his math abilities. They did, however, encourage his math, played math games with him, and regularly spoke to him about math activities.

About halfway through Billy's kindergarten year, as his reading continued its slow progress, his parents met with his teacher and discussed the difference between Billy's reading and math skills. As a result of this meeting, the teacher was able to provide suggestions for working with Billy. His parents started a routine of reading to their son, followed by questions related to the reading material. They would occasionally ask him, "Do you know what this word means?" Because he was bright, Billy's parents were reading books to him that were fairly sophisticated for a child of his age. They would talk to him about words, point to words in the text, explain them, and encourage Billy to look at the text himself and try to read various words.

Their son began to progress. He had a strong visual memory, which helped him in math, so he was learning and beginning to remember certain words. He began to point out some of the simple sight words that children first learn—little ones—such as *and*, *the*, and *ball*. His parents learned that they should be very encouraging and very supportive whenever Billy did that.

By the end of kindergarten Billy was developing sight vocabulary of words that he could read and remember. This continued in first grade, where his math continued to develop far ahead of first-grade level. His reading had improved but he continued to plod along more slowly, roughly at average level. His parents met with the teacher again. She stressed the important of continuing the reading program at home and said that she felt it was helping Billy.

An important ingredient in the process was Billy's parents' recognition of the comparative differences among his math, reading, and spelling skills.

You should remember that if your child is motivated to learn something, he can compensate for deficiencies. For example, although Billy's reading was usually at grade level, when he wanted to learn to do new magic tricks for his friends, he'd often read very sophisticated instructions and just pick out key words. He was more motivated because he enjoyed doing magic tricks. It was a chance to perform, and his friends were impressed. When Billy's parents were not available to help him learn how to do a new magic trick, he would simply sit down and read the directions himself and was able to get through them well enough to understand how to do the trick. That provided a very rewarding experience with reading. As Billy repeats that experience—reading something himself and realizing that there's some value attached to it—he will tend to read with more enthusiasm.

The Difference Between Ability Training and Academic Practice

When you help your child compensate for a particular area of weakness by further developing and applying an existing strength, you will notice there's a difference between what is called ability training and academic practice. If your child is strong in a certain subject, you can expose him to more academic material in that area. You can offer additional books and involve the child in activities available through local libraries and museums. Similarly, when your child has weaknesses, you can try to teach him academically—encourage him to catch up and make more progress.

Sometimes, however, your child may respond better to ability training, which involves teaching the basic, underlying *perceptual skill* needed to make progress. For example, eight-year-old Janice is not doing well in arithmetic and has struggled with it for quite a while. In her first few years of school her interest in math and her grades in that subject lagged behind her reading, spelling, and other language skills. Her parents tried to teach her math through academic practice—doing her homework with her, giving her extra help, and using a wide variety of approaches such as flash cards and writing down problems. Despite these efforts, Janice still had a great deal of difficulty with math.

Janice's parents and teacher decided to try to help her learn better visual skills instead of focusing directly on math. Using this approach, you should look for something your child enjoys doing related to the general area that is giving him problems. Janice's mother discovered mazes for her to do. Mazes have nothing to do directly with school, but finding her way through the puzzles helped teach Janice fine motor coordination, building one move on another, and planning ahead. Janice's parents taught her the game Battleship, which is a visual problem-solving game. It also involves sequencing, logical thinking, and developing a visual map of where the opponent's boats are located on the board. Obviously, Janice's parents were not directly teaching math skills but they were encouraging some of the visual skills that help math development. Teaching this way is more fun for the child than repeated, dogged work in his area of weakness.

Another alternative is a game called Memory, using the actual game or simply a deck of cards. This requires using visual memory and visual problem solving. If your child has verbal strengths, you can talk about your own strategy and reasoning as you play these games. In Battleship, for example, you might say, "I just made a hit at location 4F. That must mean the ship is either at 4G or 3F, so I'll try. . . ." In this way you are demonstrating your strategy and thinking out loud with your child. You also can instruct your child in making his moves. But this must be done with sensitivity. Making it more of an academic exercise may take the fun out of it for the child and thus defeat your purpose.

If you have a child who doesn't like to read or spell, you can try Tongue Twisters. This game teaches auditory sequencing—putting sounds in the right order and getting words in the right order. It will also help your child learn and remember new words and how they sound. The game is fun because players make humorous mistakes.

All of these games have a lot to do with the building blocks of reading and spelling. Another simple teaching game is Sentence Chains, which can be played at home or even in the car. Each person provides a sentence for a story. Players have to remember what the previous sentence was and add to the story, sentence by sentence. It can be goofy and silly, but the game requires some creativity. Making up sentences gives children a chance to develop memory and concept skills. Another game is Geography. Players use names of places, and the last letter of one word becomes the first letter of the next person's place word. This teaches memory, auditory sequencing, geography, and spelling skills. These various games teach or strengthen underlying skills that your child can later apply to his schoolwork.

HELPFUL HINT #7—HELP YOUR CHILD COPE WITH MISTAKES

One of the most important things you can do, once you understand your child's strengths and weaknesses, is to adopt a positive attitude about mistakes. Mistakes are OK—they're to be expected, and they're the way people learn. Your child should be helped to understand, for example, that making mistakes on homework or on tests is not fatal. Mistakes provide an opportunity to learn more and to find out what he doesn't know. Too frequently parents feel—and tell their child—that mistakes are bad and indicate irreversible failure.

Given the high level of competitiveness in our society, it's often difficult to generate a patient and tolerant attitude about mistakes. Your child may have a teacher who isn't very tolerant of mistakes even though you and your child may feel mistakes are good learning opportunities. This could make for a difficult year for the child. A teacher-parent conference is called for.

Peer pressure also can be difficult. Peers often laugh at and embarrass each other when mistakes are made. Acceptance of mistakes should be instilled early in your child. You can be a positive force in counteracting intense peer pressure. This is particularly true when your child is young and you are the primary source of values and attitudes. You can say, "It's all right if you made a mistake. I know you're trying. Mistakes are a good way to learn." When your child learns this type of positive attitude, he believes in himself. When he does make a mistake, he thinks, "OK, I made a mistake. What went wrong? How can I do this better the next time around? What do I need to learn? How can I improve?" instead of "I made a mistake. I'm dumb. What's the matter with me? There I go, I did it again. I just want to give up." A child who is able to accept mistakes from himself and others will be more likely to say to his peers when he is teased by them, "Look, I made a mistake. So what?" He may still be embarrassed and uncomfortable about it, but he'll be able to defend himself and feel he's basically OK.

The younger your child, the more influence you have in helping him feel good about himself. Obviously, you have to accept your own mistakes before you can react positively to your child's errors.

HELPFUL HINT #8—BE FLEXIBLE

If there is more than one child in your family, it's especially important for you to realize that each is different. It's important to recognize the strengths and weaknesses of each child and to adjust your expectations for each one. You should try to understand each child's strengths and weaknesses. You should support strengths and plan ways to help your child cope with weaknesses. Be aware that the real danger is that you will fall into pressuring your child or being too critical in the areas of weakness. You should keep an open mind and realize that no child can be a mirror image of his mother or father (even though he may bear a strong physical resemblance to one of you) and that each child is different.

It's important that you be flexible in your expectations. Children will develop at their own rate, and you can be most helpful by being flexible and by taking an interest in your child's areas of enjoyment, even though they may not be your own.

HELPFUL HINT #9—PROVIDE ENCOURAGEMENT

It's essential to be aware of your child's successes and to encourage them. Provide praise and reinforcement within the family for those successes. Never take them for granted. There are too many parents who look at a report card and take all the *A*s and *B*s for granted. The *C*s become the focus of attention. Such parents tend to focus on weakness because they're worried about how their child is doing. They don't want their child to suffer failures and difficulties.

Because it is a habit for many of us adults to focus on our own areas of weakness and difficulty, it is easy for us to transfer that to our children. Sometimes it's difficult to pay attention to and appreciate a child's special strengths and accomplishments, and far too many parents focus too much on a child's weaknesses.

This is true of Brent's parents. Brent is eleven years old and in sixth grade. He's capable of doing very sophisticated social studies projects. Typically he goes to the library, does some reading beyond encyclopedias, checks out books, and pulls together a fairly extensive report about, say, the geography of Australia. In his enthusiasm he compiles ten pages of written material. Brent then asks his mother for assistance. Unfortunately, she pays too much attention to the mechanics of his writing, spelling, and grammar. What happens is a project that was interesting and pleasurable becomes a source of frustration and failure because Brent's mother is applying unrealistic standards rather than understanding her child's interests and abilities.

A more positive approach would be for Brent's mother to ask him what specific help he wants, if any. Maybe he simply wants help with spelling and nothing else. Maybe he just wants praise for his effort. If Brent wants or needs help only in a specific area, it would be a good idea for her to leave the rest of the project alone.

Don't be like Brent's mother. Establish with your child in what areas he wants help and where you're going to give it. When your child isn't articulate and says only, "I want you to help me write my ideas down," you can ask, "What do you mean? Do you want to dictate to me? Do you want me to help you think out the sentences you're trying to form? What kind of writing help would you like?" Your child might answer that he doesn't know. Then you can try a single approach for a brief period of time. You might let the child dictate or help with spelling. See what happens. Again, the key is flexibility and encouragement when he does well. Try to keep your help and advice limited. Do not try to tackle the entire task of writing an extensive report all at once.

Stop and think about it. Your child is, say, eleven years old, and this is the first major report he's written—or it may be his sixth major report. What is reasonable to expect?

Remember as he goes through school that there are many more years that will provide him with the opportunity to learn and further develop skills to write reports. In his first or even his sixth report, he's not going to turn out a perfect product. Making mistakes is a way of learning. A young child's report will generally be rough. There may be problems with sentence structure and organization. That's what the teacher is there for. It's not your job to make sure there are no mistakes. When you attempt to do that, the experience can be so frustrating and negative for your child that he won't want to ask you for help again. He's not likely to involve you the next time he has a major report to complete.

A child's self-esteem may suffer if you become too involved or overly critical. Unfortunately, some parents can become so intensely involved in their child's project that they end up almost doing the report for the child. In effect, such parents are saying, "I'll do it for you because whatever you're capable of isn't good enough." This makes the child feel bad about his abilities. We've all heard stories of the proverbial school Science Fair when parents clear their calendars so they can work on their child's project. It's not unusual to hear one parent asking another, "The teacher gave us a *B* on the science report. What grade did she give you?" To which the other "helpful" parent is likely to answer, "I must have had better spelling. She gave us an *A*."

You do not really help by doing homework for your child. You'll do much better, and so will he, if you allow him to try it himself. This gives him the opportunity to learn how it feels to succeed or fail on his own efforts. Try to explain to your child that you think he is entirely capable of doing a project and that you're there only to answer questions or provide assistance. Children who learn to depend on their parents to get their work done or to get good grades can look forward to serious problems in the future.

HELPFUL HINT #10—PROVIDE STRUCTURE

Some children do not require a great deal of organization in order to do very well in school, either in the classroom or when doing their homework. They're motivated to get their work done. These are often high achievers who don't need much direction from parents or teachers. Other children need more help. They require daily attention and encouragement from their parents to do their homework during a specific time, or to practice a musical instrument, or to develop a sports skill. They need to do their work in a quiet, consistent place so that distractions don't become a problem. Often, however, as we've noted, parents can become too concerned and confuse the idea of providing structure with actually doing the work for the child. Be wary of getting into this type of situation.

This does not mean that you do not need to think carefully about routine and scheduling. Helping to establish routines for your child can only benefit him. Adjust things as you go. You may want to try to do different things until you find something that works. Here are some things to think about:

● *Place*—Most children do better with their homework if they're in a quiet place, where there's good lighting and ventilation. Working in a room with the TV on or a radio blaring can be very distracting.

● *Time*—Children do better work when they're not overly tired or hungry. Many children require time to come home, relax, have a snack, go outside, and play. If your child is active, being in school all day where he must behave and listen to the teacher can be very demanding. After school, many children will have a lot of pent-up energy that they need to release before they can sit down to do homework. Remember, however, this varies from child to child. Some children do well if they have a snack and sit down right away to get their homework finished so they have the entire evening for play and other activities. Others need to get the play out of the way before they can begin their studies. In either case, parents can often be frustrated by the negotiations that can be required to establish home study time. The following is a brief view of how one mother made time for homework even though her child wanted to be involved in other activities.

Mom: *Sasha, I see you have a lot of homework. You can't do it lying there on the floor while you're watching TV. When are you going to do it?*

Sasha: *I'll do it soon, Mom. I just want to watch the end of this program.*

Mom: *OK, but you said that last night, and I hope you remember that Aunt Gert is coming to dinner tonight.*

[Twenty minutes later, the television program is over.]

Mom: *Sasha, it's time for dinner. Aunt Gert and your little brother are too hungry to wait any longer. You'll have to do your homework when we're finished.*

Sasha: *Oh, Mom, I want to do it now. Later there's a TV show I want to watch.*

Mom: *Well, you really should have done it before. I'm sorry, you're just going to have to do it* *whenever you can after we finish supper.*

[As a result of this encounter—a variation of which routinely occurs between the two—Sasha's mother decides that she must make some changes in the way the family approaches homework.]

Mom (After school): *Sasha, we're going to start something new.*

Sasha: *Oh, yeah? What?*

Mom: *We're going to have some rules about homework, and every night we're going to try to follow the same schedule.*

Sasha: *What do you mean, Mom?*

Mom: *Well, for one thing, I don't want you to do your work in front of the television. It's hard to really concentrate. And for another, I want you to do it every day at approximately the same time. Now, when do you think you'd rather do your homework—every day right after school or right after dinner?*

Sasha: *Gosh, Mom, I don't know. Each day is so different.*

Mom: *I know, but I want to decide on a routine. After you're used to doing it that way, when something unusual comes up we can change it. But homework is very important, and that should come before TV.*

Sasha: *OK. I think I'd rather do it after dinner. But does that mean every night?*

Mom: *Yes, especially when you're first getting started. I'll help you remember, and I'll help you get started by making sure you have all the things you need to do your work.*

*[It's always a good idea to check that your child
    has the necessary supplies to actually do the
    work.]*

Ideally, you should start slowly in checking on
your child's schoolwork. You may want to ask about
what homework assignments were given, when
they're due, and how he plans to get the work done.
Then you can help him plan how he's going to do
what needs to be done. And then get out of the way
and see what happens. Does the child follow
through? Do you have to insist? Does he respond to
praise or reprimands? *The idea is to get a system in
place and working. Refinement can come later.*

With a first-grader, you might say, "What's your
homework for tonight? What's your homework for
the week?" and then take a look at it together. Next
you would probably want to ask, "OK, which subject
are you going to do first? When are you going to do
it? Do you have everything you need?" Then you
must check to see if the child does his work. If not,
you will have to step in at the time the child said he
was going to be working and ask, "Are you doing
your homework now? It's time to do your homework." Help the child get started and then leave.
Watch to see how much help he needs. The level of
support will often depend on the subject. If it's an
area of interest and strength, your child may need
very little coaching. If it's a weaker subject, you
should be prepared to offer more help.

It is important, however, to slowly reduce your
involvement after you feel the child understands
what to do. For example, Danielle is seven. She must

do one book report a week, and she doesn't enjoy doing them. She finds them frustrating, even agonizing, and therefore has trouble getting started and often can't complete once she starts.

Sure enough, at the end of one week Danielle's parents received a note from her teacher informing them that Danielle failed to do her book report the previous week and that she'd had trouble completing them for the last several weeks. The teacher also sent home an unfinished report. Danielle's parents sat down with her to complete what she hadn't finished. They quickly realized that Danielle doesn't read very well on her own and doesn't enjoy it. Her parents were vaguely aware of this problem, but not that it was causing Danielle so much difficulty. With the agreement of her teacher, Danielle's parents read the required book to her so she could at least prepare a report, even if she really didn't read the book herself.

This way Danielle managed to complete her required reports for three weeks in a row. A few weeks later Danielle's mother chose a very simple book for her to read by herself. Then she chose a more difficult book about the solar system because Danielle was very interested in stars and was able to get the gist of it even though she couldn't understand all the words. Eventually, as she became more successful, doing reports became less difficult and Danielle was able to do them on her own.

Often, parents expect the transition that Danielle eventually made to take place more quickly. In fact, it may take several weeks to a few months for you to gradually shift all the work over to your child and have less involvement. It's a step-by-step process. So be prepared for some stop and go, taking a few steps forward and maybe a few back.

Unfortunately, the way you teach a child about responsibility with homework is through sometimes painful experience. When it's bedtime and an assignment hasn't been done, your child should still observe bedtime. It doesn't matter why the assignment was not done. It may be because the child has avoided it and put it off until the last minute or because he watched a special television show instead. In any case, it may be necessary for him to get up early the next morning to finish it or to take it into school unfinished. *You must be willing to allow your child to experience frustration and small degrees of failure so that he can learn the importance of routine, planning, and structure.* Many parents have trouble letting their children do that. They will decide that what is required is for the child to stay up until 10:00 or 11:00 to finish the assignment. They do not want the child to go to school the next day with the work incomplete. Children don't learn from that experience, even when the parent insists that this is the last time this is going to be allowed. Instead the child learns how to ensure that he can stay up until 10:30 or 11:00 again to complete the work.

It's essential that your child understand that getting his work done during a specific time period is important and will make him feel better about the subject and himself. In this situation it is unwise to allow too much flexibility because then your child will never learn to face the issue head on.

HELPFUL HINT #11—PROVIDE A GOOD EARLY MORNING SEND-OFF

The way your child starts his day at home carries over to the way his time will be spent at school. An uneventful morning routine is helpful and very important. A child who arrives at school feeling rested and having eaten breakfast will feel good and will be prepared to get involved in the day's activities. The more demanding the family schedule is, the more difficult it is to arrange this type of start for the day, but it is important. When both parents are working, or when there's more than one child in the family, or when the children go to different schools and are in different carpools, logistics become complicated and require more planning. It's very difficult for some parents to be able to provide this kind of structure for their children because it's difficult for them to do it for themselves. It takes tremendous cooperation and effort between you and your child; but if your child regularly arrives at school unprepared to start the day, he's already at a disadvantage, and his academic development is bound to suffer.

Teachers can easily spot a child who is not ready to face the day. The child may seem tired, agitated, or just not "with it." If this type of situation continues on a regular basis, the alert teacher will discuss it with the parents. But you shouldn't count on this happening. Obviously, problems at home will have an influence on your child. You should be aware of this and try to take care of your difficulties in a way that keeps the child's welfare in mind.

HELPFUL HINT #12—HELP YOUR CHILD FEEL GOOD ABOUT HIMSELF

You should work to raise your child's self-esteem whenever possible. Understand and accept relative weaknesses so that your child feels good enough about himself to do well in areas of strength. Your child's sense of self-esteem is a prime factor in his success—academically and otherwise.

When you speak to your child, whether it be to praise him or discuss something significant, the most important thing to remember is to be brief. Long-winded explanations don't work with young children. When parents use words that are far beyond a child's ability, they will just lose the child's attention. He won't want to listen.

It's important to think about what you want to say ahead of time. You might even want to rehearse it in your own mind. You can also help your child by praising him whenever you have the chance. Maybe your child is of average intelligence, but he's kind and very popular. Praising him for his good traits, even in areas that aren't academic, makes him feel good about himself and encourages him to perform at his peak. You can also say, "That was a terrific art project you did," or "You're so quick with learning subtraction." Be sure to praise your child's successes. This makes him feel capable and enhances his self-esteem.

If your child is having difficulty in school, it's crucial to do other things that you can enjoy together.

Ideally, these should be activities that are not related to school, such as cooking, gardening, sports, and exercise. This also helps your child feel good. Enjoying hiking, camping, dancing, or music together are other possibilities. It's tragic when parents focus only on a child's difficulties. Sometimes the situation becomes so serious that everything in the home focuses on the child's troubles. *You should do everything in your power to do things as a family that give you a chance to praise and enjoy your child.*

Emphasize the positive not the negative. This will give your child the feeling he does have solid attributes and the ability to improve. If you harp on poor performance, it will become more and more magnified in the child's mind. It is important that your child feel he has abilities that are valued.

HELPFUL HINT #13—SUPPORT YOUR CHILD'S INTERESTS

If your child shows interest in a special area at school, there are usually activities outside of school that can enhance those interests. It might be Little League, dance classes, art classes, computer classes, or reading clubs at the local library. By the time children are in the upper grades there are often what are called enrichment clubs at school. There may be a chess club or a science club or Girl Scouts and Boy Scouts. All are important and offer valuable experience for your child to build on his interests and strengths.

Many public schools are cutting back on extracurricular activities because of budget restrictions. In some schools educators are responding to pressure to emphasize reading, writing, and arithmetic skills. In these cases outside programs can provide the child with some of the learning activities that previously were found in school. There are many places to find such activities—YMCA, church groups, the local parks and recreation department, and private classes. These activities encourage your child to expand his skills and develop new areas of expertise.

Early activities like these may provide the spark for a future career. There are many scientists who started their careers with a small chemistry set or by participating in an after-school science club. However, these types of activities can become stressful when they're not matched to a child's areas of interest. You should never try to push your child into something just because you think it might help him later. And children should not be cajoled into an activity just because all the bright kids in school are involved or because he is weak in an area and you hope the extra activity will shake him out of the problem.

You should keep in mind that there is a limit to the number of activities and hours that can be imposed on a child outside of school. Be happy if your child is involved with only one or two projects that interest him. Don't force him into activities because his friend next door is involved. Determine what your child's areas of interest and skills are and point him gently in those directions. Enjoying one or two activities is better than coasting along and disliking several that don't mean anything to him.

HELPFUL HINT #14 — KNOW ABOUT YOUR CHILD'S ACADEMIC ENVIRONMENT

In many schools parents have some input about selecting their children's teachers. The qualities of a good teacher change as the child gets older. For younger children, kindergarten and first and second grades are a time for learning social skills and adapting to school. Therefore, it's very important that the teacher be warm, encouraging, and able to relate well to your child. The classroom should be set up with varied reinforcements and rewards for required activities. These might be stars for getting homework in on time or tokens for good behavior. There should be various types of activities that involve seeing, hearing, and sensory skills, what is called multisensory learning. It's especially crucial for parents of children entering kindergarten and first grade to visit the classroom before the first day of school. If there are several choices of teachers, you should sit in each class for just a few minutes to see what the atmosphere is like.

The early educational experiences of a child are crucial. If your child has a successful experience early on, he'll have a better chance for success as he progresses through school. In second grade, for example, it's important to visit the class, but probably not as important as in kindergarten. Some schools and principals are open to parent visits. In fact, many schools regularly schedule open houses when all the teachers are available and the children's classroom work is on display. Most teachers in these grades will make time to visit with parents individually to discuss a child's progress. In a few cases, however, schools and principals may not be as responsive. You have to feel your way. Most schools are open to and tolerant of parental observation and input because in the long run it makes the teacher's job easier.

The other important part of understanding the academic environment is knowing your child. Based on what the child has experienced in preschool or in early elementary school years, you can usually develop an understanding of what your child's strengths are, what kind of adults teach your child successfully, and what kind of classroom setting is good for your child. Some children do better in a highly organized classroom where there are formal lessons and a predictable schedule, the teacher focuses on the class as a group, and students are expected to keep up. Some children are used to this type of structure and get distracted when there are changes in the routine.

Other children do very well in a looser situation where there's more variety, less routine, and more self-motivated projects. Such children achieve well in learning centers and with self-paced activities. Knowing how your child responds at home, you will understand the type of environment in which your child does best. Some children respond better to either a male or a female teacher. Some children do better with a high-energy teacher; others work better with slower-paced, more relaxed people.

It's often possible for you to make choices in terms of classroom structure. Lacking these choices, you can assist your child in adapting by discussing the situation with the teacher and the child. Remember, flexibility is important. It's not always possible for your child to have the ideal learning environment. Look for ways to improve the situation and try to understand the reasons for your child's problems.

Helping a Child Who Is Bored in School

A child who is bored in school is frequently not getting enough stimulation. Perhaps he is not being offered enough challenges. The work may be too simple, repetitive, and mundane. Your child may be capable of more than what's expected of him. Such children are usually above average, with special talents and abilities in certain areas, but they find themselves in a rather average group where the teacher isn't providing enough enrichment and individualized attention to the more gifted child.

This is the type of situation in which it's important to meet with the teacher to see what type of individualized instruction is available. Can subgroupings within the classroom be formed? Can your child be grouped with children from other classes? Frequently, reading programs are established across classroom lines where children are grouped according to ability. Sometimes this also occurs with math and science groups.

It is also true, however, that sometimes a child is bored because he's not capable of doing the work required of him. It could be that your child is over his head in the class. If he is relatively quiet and passive—one who may not have a behavioral problem in the class—he may be bored because the work is too difficult. Again, consultation with the teacher becomes important to determine what your child is capable of. Sometimes teachers can do a brief assessment of the child or they can recommend that the school psychologist do an evaluation to see exactly what the child's potential is.

You might also want to personally observe your child in class. First, of course, you must obtain the teacher's permission to visit, ideally three or four times, especially at the time when your child is frequently bored. You should note what lessons are being taught and how your child responds. Your child might be better behaved when you're there, but it is an important beginning. Next, talk with the teacher and the principal to see what other possibilities exist in the school. See if the child should be placed in another group. It's not easy to do, and teachers are sometimes reluctant to attempt things on a trial basis, but if you are firm, you may be successful. If it's a persistent problem, and the child is doing OK otherwise, it might be a good idea to consider changing teachers. Or if the problem is especially bad, and school personnel are unresponsive, you might think about changing schools. When evaluating that possibility, make sure you take time to judge the existing school adequately—you don't want to go from the frying pan into the fire.

If the problem persists, the school is unresponsive, you are unable to change schools, or your child seems to be troubled by more than just his schoolwork, then you should probably seek professional help outside of the school district—a licensed family therapist or child psychologist recommended to you, if possible.

Choosing a School

Schools have different programs. Depending on the director and the teaching staff—whether private or public—each school has a different philosophy. Private schools, especially, may differ greatly from one another. Some are more academic. Others are more social. Some are academic with unusual approaches to teaching and learning. Some are more structured, others more free-form. Some emphasize reading and language arts whereas others specialize in math and sciences. Parochial schools emphasize religious, cultural, and social values. Size of classrooms, teacher-to-student ratio, homogeneity of the students, and variety of facilities are factors involved in choosing a school. You need to evaluate all of these carefully. Choosing a school is an important and fundamental decision and may have significant long-term effects on your child.

When the type of teacher you want for your child isn't available, you have the difficult task of selecting the best of the ones who are available. Work with the teacher as much as possible. You can look for outside activities to stimulate your child if the classroom situation is undesirable. Sometimes it's a question of surviving that year, getting as much out of it as possible, and waiting for the following year to obtain a more suitable teacher.

Some children do not learn very well when they don't like or feel good about the teacher. Other children learn very well as long as they're involved in areas of primary interest, regardless of the teacher. These children can still do well and learn a lot even if the teacher isn't very friendly, warm, or easygoing. Sometimes, too, if your child does well, he can actually bring out whatever warmth and encouragement that teacher is capable of giving.

There are times when you have to make difficult choices. You may have to choose a person who isn't the best teacher and sacrifice part of your child's learning experience for a short period of time. Your child may learn less than you want, but it might be worth it.

For example, Mr. and Mrs. Quinn had two teachers to choose from for their daughter, Sally. The first, Mrs. Jones, is highly structured and somewhat businesslike. Sally is sensitive and needs an encouraging, warm teacher. Her parents put her in Ms. Brownell's class, even though this teacher operates a very relaxed, less structured classroom, which is the opposite of the kind of situation Sally does well in. Ms. Brownell is very warm and easygoing, and Sally's parents decided it would be better for Sally to have emotional support, even if it meant sacrificing a little learning. In this case, Sally was able to get more involved in class and participate in classroom activities that she enjoyed. It's entirely possible that, if she were enrolled in Mrs. Jones's class, her school year would have been difficult, if not disastrous. At some later point, Sally might be ready to succeed in a more highly structured, less emotionally supportive classroom. Additionally, her parents might find that if Sally participates in activities outside of the classroom, Sally may be able to make up for some of the learning that she may miss in Ms. Brownell's room. These should be activities related to basic academic skills rather that ability training—a library reading group or a special tutorial, as long as the tutor is one who can relate to Sally's emotional needs.

As public schools strive to keep their enrollments, there are more and more school settings where parents have choices. If you have a child who has a strength in one area—math, for example—you might consider choosing a school that offers a special program in math. Some communities call these *magnet schools*. But you should be wary of too much specialization in one subject. Whatever school you choose should also be strong in all areas of basic subjects, including reading and language arts. Reading-related activities, especially, shouldn't play second fiddle.

We have come to something that reflects current trends in our competitive society—specialization. We have somehow convinced ourselves that to achieve our goals we must first put ourselves in the hands of a specialist. As a result, there is a lack of people who are well-rounded in education and elsewhere. Our technically oriented culture is producing more and more individuals who have narrow interests and abilities—people who are highly skilled in one particular area and almost totally incompetent in others. *One of the best gifts you can give your young child is the opportunity to investigate and experiment with many interests in his early years, so that when he does make a career choice, he can do so freely and with a fundamental knowledge of his preferred interests and abilities.*

CONCLUSION

If you have learned one thing from this book, we hope it is that you must actively be involved in your child's academic development. If you are not, not only will your child most likely suffer, but you yourself will be missing out on a lot of the fun and rewards of parenting. More important, you won't really know what kind of student—and potential citizen—your child is.

Think of all the surprises you can avoid if you are informed about what your child is doing in school. No notes from the teacher saying that Suzie can't read, that Johnny disrupts the class, or that April falls asleep at her desk. Your child needs and wants your help and guidance. When he becomes a teenager, he may elect to ignore much of what you tell him (or, at least, pretend to do so).

The elementary school age is your opportunity to

establish your family strategies for helping your child do well in school. Make time for this activity, because it will be sure to pay dividends in later years. Too many parents of teenagers who are having trouble in school find themselves saying, "I wish I had paid more attention to my child when he was younger—maybe he wouldn't be failing now."

The advice provided in this book is based on many years of professional observation and counsel with children like yours. Some cases are more difficult than others, but the general rules are the same. Remember, as we have said repeatedly throughout this book, that the most important requirements for maximizing your child's academic potential are your time, interest, concern, and love.

As we've suggested, companion books in this series that provide additional information on this subject include *Creating a Good Self-Image in Your Child*, about the challenge of the tasks children encounter as they grow up, *When Your Child Isn't Doing Well in School*, which is concerned particularly with underachieving children who are experiencing academic difficulties, and *When Your Child Grows Up Too Fast*, which deals with children who are influenced to perform beyond their age and ability.

REFERENCES

Beck, Joan. *How to Raise a Brighter Child.* New York: Pocket Books, 1975.

Becker, Wesley C. *Parents Are Teachers.* Champaign, IL: Research Press, 1971.

Lewis, David. *You Can Teach Your Child Intelligence.* New York: Berkley Books, 1984.

Musser, Paul; Conger, John; and Kagan, Jerome. *Child Development and Personality,* fifth edition. New York: Harper and Row, 1979.

Simpson, Eileen. *Reversals, a Personal Account of Victory Over Dyslexia.* New York: Washington Square Press, 1979.

Parents can also contact local colleges' Departments of Education for information on local associations for gifted children, learning disabled children, and other special needs.